FOR DIRTY, RACIST, SEXIST MEN

MIKE ROSS

Strathearn Publishing

TRADE DISTRIBUTION

foulsham

The Publishing House, Bennetts Close,
Cippenham, Berks. SL1 5AP

strathearn publishing ltd.

PO Box 44, Slough, Berkshire, SL1 4YN

ISBN 0-572-01757-X

Copyright © 1992 M. F. Ross

Printed in Great Britain by Cox & Wyman Ltd., Reading.

Wanna be Famous?

Wanna be an Author?

Just Send us a Joke!

If you hear a funny story and think that it would be good for our next collection, then just send it in.

If we publish *your* joke in the next book, we will acknowledge you as its author and send you a free copy containing your name in print.

You can then flash the book 'round the pub to show how famous you have become. And insist that those who wish to remain in your company buy you drinks in recognition of your achievement!

Yours for a laugh.

ED.
Strathearn Publishing

P.S. You'll find our address on the back of the title page. Where we have more than one submission of the same joke, then it will be the first received which will be given the credit.

5

"I never drink water.
Fish fuck in it!"

Some real headlines:

EIGHTH ARMY PUSH BOTTLES UP GERMANS!

DR. FUCHS OFF TO ANTARCTICA!

Somebody is supposed to have said, to one of England's most famous cricketers:
"Do you know Fred, you've got a big arse for a fast bowler."
To which the bowler is said to have replied:
"You can't knock in a tent peg with a tack hammer!"

*A man came home
extremely angry and said
to his wife:*

*"I've just been down the pub
talking to our bloody milkman.
The cheeky bastard says He's
fucked every woman in this
street except one."*

*"Must be that stuck up bitch
at number five,"
said his wife.*

A white man, stood in a gents toilet, started to glance down at the cock of the black guy who was standing next to him.

"M... he exclaimed. "...said how do you blo...s ...to get such big ...es"

"Well, said the black man. When ...are young out ...others ...a piece of ...ring to our tool, and the... they attach a heavy stone to the string. Eventually ...al stretches our cocks."

A Frenchman returned to his hotel room in London.
He opened a connecting door to the next room.
He saw a beautiful blonde lying on her back
with her legs wide open.

Later that night when he was asleep
in his own room
the door burst open and he was dragged
out of bed by the police.

But Messieurs! What is zees all about?"

"The woman next door has been dead since six o'clock
and she's lying next to your wallet!"

"But Monsieur, this cannot be true,
we made love at ten o'clock."

"Are you telling me that you deliberately fucked
a woman who had been dead for four hours?"

"Non Monsieur, I did not know she was dead,
I just thought she was English!"

Q. **What prevents Australians from manufacturing penicillin?**

A. **No known culture has ever been able to survive there!**

I **HATE** THIS KIND OF LANGUAGE —YOU KNOW THAT!

9

A footballer had been having a hard time
with the referee.
Another yellow card was the last straw.

"I suppose if I called you a cunt you'd send
me off?" He demanded.
"I'd have to," said the Ref.
The footballer considered for a moment.
"If I only *thought* you were a cunt, you
couldn't do anything could you?"
"No," admitted the Ref.
"In that case, I *think* you're a cunt!"

Q. What's the definition
of an Irishman?

A. A simple machine
for converting
Guinness
into piss!

10

An ideal Europe is where:
The cooks are French
The police are British
The engineers are German
The lovers are Italian
and everything is organised by the Swiss

A nightmare Europe is where:
The cooks are British
The police are German
The engineers are French
The lovers are Swiss
and everything is organised by the Italians.

Abie went into the synagogue and prayed.
"God, you've got to make me win the sweepstake.
I'm desperate. I owe money to everybody!
Next week he was back.
"God," he said.
"If I don't win the synagogue sweepstake this week,
I'm a ruined man.
Suddenly a big voice boomed from the sky:
"Abie! Please!
Meet me half way.
Buy a ticket!!"

11

**Did you hear about the Chinese
couple who got a divorce;
She went back to Peking,
and he went back to Wanking!**

A Catholic priest, an Anglican vicar and a Rabbi were discussing what they did with their collection money.

"I weigh it," said the vicar. Then I divide it; half for God and half for me."

"I count it out," said the priest. "One for me, one for God, one for me, one for God, and so on."

"Me," said the Rabbi? "I take it into the middle Temple and I throw it all up in the air. What God wants, he keeps; and what comes back down is mine!"

This one is just too tasteless. Ed.

**Fighting
for peace
is a bit like
Fucking
for virginity!**

q. Why do Australians whistle when they have a shit?

a. So they know which end to wipe!

"I've got to dash — I'm on a promise tonight.
I'm going to use the Rodeo position!"
"What the hell is the Rodeo position?"
"Well, you get her down on the bed
and start giving it to her doggy fashion.
As soon as she starts to enjoy it
you whisper in her ear
'That's how Tracy at the pub likes it.
Then you have to see how long you can stay on!"

15

An Englishman, an Irishman ... were having ... into each ... rem... CENSORED ... it on the ... ...ed his— and ... after ... a week, he had dented seventeen.

Q. How do you know when you've upset the barmaid?

A. When you find a string hanging out of your Bloody Mary.

AND THIS SHOULD HAVE BEEN CENSORED TOO!

Confucious he say:
"Secretary, like typewriter;
not part of office furniture
'till screwed to desk.

Q. *How do you confuse an Irishman?*
A. *Show him three shovels and tell
him to take his pick!*

**Then there was the Irishman
who thought that
'genitalia' was an Italian airline
and that
'cunnilingus' flew from Ireland.**

Q. **What is the difference between Italians and a piece of buttered toast?**

A. **You can make soldiers out of the toast.**

18

The guest speaker at the Women's Institute had difficulty in remembering names.
He had particular trouble with the President's name; Mrs Franny.
"Just remember, it's Fanny with an 'R'."
Said one of the helpful ladies.
At the end of the speech the speaker said:
"I want to thank you ladies for your interest and especially your President ... Mrs Crunt!"

A white man, stood in a gents toilet, ~~chanced~~ to ~~glance down at the~~ ~~[...]~~ who was standing ~~[...]~~.

"M~~[...]~~ he exclaimed in admiration. "How do you blokes manage to get such ~~[...]~~ ones?"

"~~[...]~~ said the black man. When w~~[...]~~ our ~~[...]~~ ~~[...]~~ string ~~[...]~~ our tool, and the~~[...]~~ a ~~heavy~~ stone to the string. Eventually that stretches our cocks."

"~~[...]~~ I think I'll try that!" announced the white man ~~[...]~~

A couple of ~~[...]~~ ~~[...]~~ the same toilet.

19

Q. *What's the difference between a bad hunter and a constipated owl?*

A. *One shoots and can't hit.*
The other hoots and can't ...

Q. How can you tell when a politician is lying?

A. When his lips move.

Q. Why did God give negros rhythm?

A. Because he fucked up their hair.

Quantas Pilot:

"Ladies and gentlemen, we will shortly be landing in Auckland, New Zealand. Please set your watches back twenty-five years."

20

Confucious he say:
"Honourable woman aviator who fly upside down, have crack up!"

Did you hear about the woman who went to sleep on the synagogue steps? Woke up with a heavy Jew on her.

A blind man was waiting to cross the road,
when his guide dog pissed on his leg.
He reached into his pocket
and took out a biscuit for the dog.
A passer-by, who had seen everything remarked:
"That's very tolerant of you after what he just did."
"Not really," came the reply.
"I'm just finding out where his mouth is.
So that I can kick him in the balls!"

21

The young barmaid was ████████████████ street
when she ████████████████████ small boys
████████████ the ████████████.
"What's this ████████████?" she asked ████
"It's a ████████████," replied the boy.
"Oh, said the barmaid, ████████████?"
"████████████, said the boy, ████████████."

Taking out his prick he rubbed ~~cheerful erection and then slapped~~ proudly ~~rick he rubbed it~~ "There yo~~it onto the table;~~ "A clear w~~ts length on the~~ "'fraid not~~dlord," he said.~~ "You see all~~t you think?"~~ other side of~~said the landlord,~~ They all put t~~all our blokes do it from~~ the winner tak~~other side of the table!"

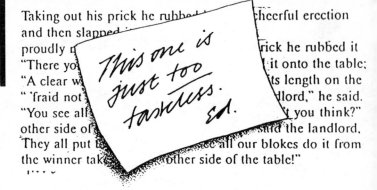

This one is just too tasteless. Ed.

"You're taking a long time to come tonight darling!"

"Yes, I can't think of anyone exciting!"

Some geologists working in northern Canada needed more equipment and sent a cable to their head office:

'SEND THREE PUNTS AND A CANOE STOP.'

The reply came quickly:

'THREE GIRLS ARRIVING SOON STOP BUT WHAT IS A PANOE?' STOP

23

Little boy: "Look at this!
You haven't got one of THESE!"

Little girl: "No, but I've got one of
THESE and my big sister says that one
of THESE will get as many of THOSE
as I want!"

Q. **Why don't Italians have freckles?**
A. **They slide off.**

Q. What does HMS mean
on a British Warship?
A. Her Majesty's Ship.

Q. What does USS mean
on an American warship?
A. United States Ship.

Q. What does AMB mean
on an Italian warship?
A. Assa Ma Boata!

Q. **What do you call a beautiful girl in Poland?**

A. **A tourist.**

> *You will have to wait,*
> *I can only deal with*
> *one shit at a time.*
>
> (Lord Beaverbrook - from a lavatory cubicle)

25

Q. What's the difference between a cross-country run and a kitchen maid.

A. Well, ones a pant in the country ....

26 ▶ A Pole can not only read the bottom line of an optician's chart, he can pronounce it!

Q.

What is the only onomatapoeic city in the world?

A.

Bangkok.

"My God!" Said the nurse.
"That's the biggest prick I've ever seen.
Is it rampant or dormant?"
"It's dormant," replied the patient.
"Strewth! What's it like when it's rampant?"
"I don't know," said the man,
"I've never seen it."
"How's that?" She asked.
"Well, it takes so much blood to get it up,
I faint before it gets there!"

If they were going to give the world an enema, they'd stick the tube in New York.

27

Two ███ were ███ their ███████ when a
naked woman ███████████ and into the woods.
A couple of minutes later she ███████ two█
███████ and then ████████ bloke ███████ two
██████ s of ███
Finally followed a little ██████████ up the rear.
The two ███████████ him and ████████████ what
████ on.

A new site manager went over to Paddy
and asked him to dig a hole.
"Fuck Off!" Said Paddy.
"Now look here!" said the manager.
"You do what you are told."
"Fuck Off!" Said Paddy again.
The site manager went over to the foreman
and told him to fire Paddy.
The foreman said that Paddy was a good worker,
and that it was merely necessary to treat him right.
He went over to Paddy and hit him over the
head with a shovel.
Paddy immediately started digging.
At the end of the day, the site manager went
over to Paddy and asked why he
wouldn't do anything except for the foreman.
"Well Sorr."
"He explained it better!"

Wife:
"I wish I had a bigger pair of tits".
Husband:
"Try rubbing a piece of toilet paper
up and down between them.
Wife:
"Do you really think that would do the trick?"
Husband:
"Well, it did wonders for your arse".

29

30 *Q. What do elephants use for tampons?*
A. Sheep.

A man, walking down his local high street, noticed
that a self-service brothel had newly opened.
He decided to try out the establishment.
On entering he saw a machine, bearing the sign:
ENTRY FEE £30 -
PAY HERE AND FOLLOW THE SIGNS!

The man put his money into the slot
and a door opened, which closed again
after he had entered.
In front of him were three more doors,
marked

'EUROPEAN GIRLS', 'ASIAN GIRLS',
and 'AFRICAN GIRLS'

He went through the door marked
'EUROPEAN GIRLS'

He was confronted by another two doors,
this time marked 'BLONDES' and 'BRUNETTES'
He chose 'BLONDES'.

Ahead of him now were a further two doors:
'LARGE BREASTS' and 'SMALL BREASTS'
He chose 'LARGE BREASTS'

Once more he found two doors, this time labelled
'BIG CUNTS' and 'LITTLE CUNTS'
Thinking carefully, he entered the door
marked 'BIG CUNTS'

And found himself back in the street!

Him: "Hi there beautiful.

What's your birth sign?"

Her: "Herpes!"

Rastus: "Oooh Liza! Is I in *you* or is I in the mud?"

Liza: "I guess you'se in the mud."

Rastus: "*Now* Liza! Is I in you or is I in the mud?"

Liza: "Ooh Rastus! You'se in *me*!"

Rastus: "Well Liza I'se gonna put it back in the mud!"

A passer-by saw Paddy lying in the street, with a broken leg.
"How did you come to break your leg?"
"Oi didn't come to break my leg,
Oi came to mend the roof!"

34 *The newly weds booked into their honeymoon hotel and didn't come out of their room for three days.*

*The hotel staff were getting worried.
They had asked for no food during that period.
Eventually the manager went up to their
room and knocked on the door:*

*"Excuse me Sir, are you alright in there?"
"Yes thank you," came the reply.*

*"But Sir, how can you manage for so long
without any food?"
"We're living on the fruits of love!"*

*"Well could you please stop throwing the skins
out of the window, they're choking the chickens!"*

Q. What's the difference
between a nun and a girl
in a bath?

A. One's got a soul full of hope.
The other's got a whole . . .
Think about it!

Confucious he say:
"Man who go to bed with
sex problem on mind,
wake up with solution in hand!"

**Three surgeons were discussing their
favourite types of patient.**

**"I like operating on Germans" said the
first "everything is always beautifully
made and in the right place!"**

**"I like operating on Japanese," said the
second "it's so easy 'cos everything is
miniaturised and colour coded!"**

**"I like operating on Americans," said
the third "there are only two organs
a mouth and an arsehole
and they're interchangeable!"**

There is no homosexuality in Poland because like Poles repel each other.

Sitting on a train with a young curate,
a bishop was attempting to do
the Times crossword.
"Three across," he said out loud
"Exclusively female, four letters,
ends in 'unt'?"
"That would be 'Aunt'," suggested the curate.
"So it would," said the bishop.
"Have you an eraser by any chance?"

Sex
is the single
most common
cause of
human beings.

38

Confucious he say:
"Woman who sit on jockey's knee get red hot tip."

Olga Von Brownbread said to the team doctor; "I'm very worried about these pills you've been giving me.
I seem to be growing hairs on my chest."

The doctor asked:
"How far down do they go?"

"All the way down to my balls!"

The young barmaid was ▓▓▓▓▓▓▓▓▓▓ street
When she ▓▓▓▓▓▓▓▓▓▓▓▓▓▓▓ small boys
▓▓▓▓▓▓▓▓▓▓ ▓g the ▓▓▓▓▓▓.
"What's this ▓▓▓▓▓▓▓▓?" she asked ▓▓▓▓
▓▓▓▓.
"It's a ▓▓▓▓▓▓▓" replied the boy.
"Oh, said the barmaid, "▓▓▓▓▓▓▓▓?"
"▓▓▓▓▓▓▓▓" said the boy, "▓▓▓▓▓▓▓▓."

Irishman: "I'd like some of that there deodorant."
Shop Assistant: "Do you mean this one; the ball type?"
Irishman: "No, I want it for under my arms!"

39

Q.
How do you make an Italian?
A.
You take a lump of shit in each hand and bring them together like this.
WOP!

A fellow on his first parachute jump
pulled so hard that his rip-cord broke.
As he plummeted towards the ground,
he saw a man wearing an apron
with a can of lager in his hand.
The man was flying towards him.

"I say," said the falling bloke,
"do you know anything about parachutes?"
"No mate," said the other.
"Do you know anything
about gas powered barbecues?"

Q. *Did you hear about the Irishman who finished two weeks of study for a urine test?*

Sheilah 'Why have you got that Tampax tucked behind yer ear?"

42 ▶ "Oh shit, what 'ave I done with me fag?"

Interviewer: Tell me Stevie, what is it like being blind?"

Stevie Wonder: "Sure is better than being black!"

The bride's mother, on the eve of the wedding, told the groom "I think you have the right to know that my daughter has been to the doctor for a check-up.

He says that she has acute angina."

"He's absolutely right," agreed the man.

43

"She's got a pert little bum and a lovely pair of tits too!"

Q. **How does a Frenchwoman hold her liquour?**

A. **By the ears.**

44 ▶

The smallest book
in the world:
'Negros I have met at
the Yacht Club'

What are the four commonest lies in the
English Language?
1. **The cheque's in the mail!**
2. **Of course I'm not married!**
3. **Of course I love you!**
4. **I promise I won't come in your mouth!**

A white man, stood in a gents toilet, started to
glance down at the cock of the black guy who
was standing next to him.

"M... the ex... said and glanced
down ... long to ... ches"

"Y... said ... When we are young
our ... a piece of string to our tool, and
the they attach a heavy stone to the string.
Eventually that stretches our cocks."

The expectant father was pacing up and down
when the nurse came out and said he had a son.

A few minutes later she announced another one.
"Doesn't surprise me," he said,
"with the equipment I've got."

She reappeared again and said it was triplets.
"That's because of my huge chopper" he
exclaimed.

Out she came once more.
"It's quads!" She announced.
"Nurse, you should see this tool of mine,
it's like a chimney stack!"

"Well I'd have it swept if I were you
they're all coming out black!"

Q. Why did God make urine yellow
and sperm white?

A. So that the Irish could tell if they
were coming or going.

Q. Which Shakespeare plays do these
remind you of:
3 inch, 6 inch, 9 inch, Wet?

A. 3 inch – Much Ado About Nothing
6 inch – As You Like It
9 inch – The Taming of The Shrew
Wet – Midsummer Night's Dream

Q. What do you get if you cross a
nun with an Apple?

A. A computer that won't go down
on you!

Q. What's the quickest way to grease an Army Land-Rover?
A. Drive it over an Argentinian.

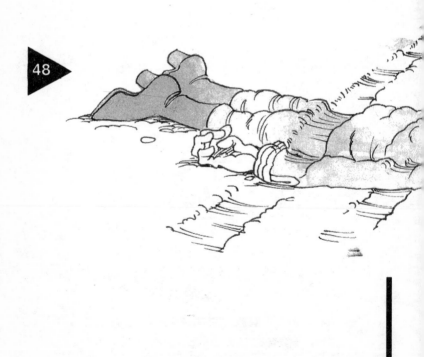

A schoolboy wrote:
"Magellan circumcised the world
with his fifty-foot clipper"

"Joan of Arc was
condomed to death."

A white man stood in a gents toilet, ~~chanced to glance down at the co~~ who was standing ~~next to him~~.

"~~M~~ he exclaimed in admiration. "How do you blokes manage to get such big ones?"

DISGUSTING

"~~Well~~" said the ~~black man~~. "When we a~~re born~~ our mothers ti~~e a piece of~~ string ~~to our tool~~, and the~~n~~ att~~ach a~~ heavy stone to the string. Eventually that stretches our cocks."

~~"D~~ ~~know~~ I think I'll try that!" announced the white ~~man~~

A couple of month~~s~~ ~~later~~ ~~the two met~~ ag~~ain in~~ the same toilet.

50

A white man, stood in a gents toilet [CENSORED] to glance down at the cock of the black guy who was standing next to him.

"M[CENSORED] he ex[CENSORED] [CENSORED] do [CENSORED] do you blo[CENSORED] [CENSORED] [CENSORED]cs"

"[CENSORED] said [CENSORED] [CENSORED]n. When [CENSORED] are young our [CENSORED] a piece of [CENSORED] to our tool, and the[CENSORED] attach [CENSORED] stone to the string. Eve[CENSORED] stretches our cocks."

A lady walked into the doctor's surgery and said:
"I have this embarrasing problem doctor.
Every time I move, my pussy whistles."
"Good Lord", said the doctor.
"I wondered what that was when you came in."
He checked her thoroughly and, there was no doubt.
Realising the impact of this discovery,
he tape recorded her whole repertoire.

Some weeks later at an important medical seminar,
he proudly revealed his discovery.
After five minutes of recorded whistles, he
addressed his audience:

"Now then gentlemen. Can anybody hazard a guess
as to the source of these sounds?"

A voice from the back piped up:
"Sounds like some cunt whistling to me!"

Q. What do you call an Irishman with half a brain?

A. Gifted.

A black man was standing in a line of whites,
waiting to vote.
A clerk at the desk was giving everyone
a literacy test.
When the black got there the clerk said.
"Can you read boy?"
"Sho can," he replied.
"Read this then," said the clerk,
handing him a Hebrew copy of the Jewish Chronicle
"I can't read the words
but I sho can read the headlines," said the black.
"Oh yeah! Well what does it say then?"
"It says, 'Ain't no niggers voting in this town today!'"

53

SEXIST

AT LAST SOME
SENSE IS
BREAKING THROUGH

Wales . . .
Where men
are men,
and the sheep
are nervous!

Q. "What's the difference between drunks and alcoholics?"

A. "We drunks don't have to go to those bloody silly meetings!"

56

Times had been tough and so the old dear told her husband that there was nothing else to do, she would have to go on the game. Off she went, and came home about eight hours later.
"How much did you make?" asked the old man.
"Twenty pounds and 50 pence," she told him.
"What miserable bastard gave you the 50 pence!" he demanded.
"All of them!"

Q. Kamikaze means 'Divine Wind' doesn't it?

A. No. It means there's a nasty Nip in the air!

The *scribbled handwritten text, crossed out, with* **Disgusting** *written over it*

A white man, stood in a gents toilet, chanced to glance down at the cock of the black guy who was standing next to him.

"M... he ex... I'm... I le down blow... you ... es"

"Y... said the ... n. When we are young ou ... tie a piece of string to our tool, and the ... attach a heavy stone to the string. Even... that stretches our cocks."

Glasgow . .
the River Clyde
is the arsehole
of Europe.
58 And Glasgow
is thirty miles
up it!

The young barmaid was ▮▮▮▮▮▮ street when she ▮▮▮▮▮▮ small boys ▮▮▮▮▮▮ the ▮▮▮▮▮▮
  "What's this ▮▮▮▮▮▮ "she asked ▮▮▮▮▮▮
  "It's a ▮▮▮▮▮▮" replied the boy.
  "Oh, said the barmaid, ▮▮▮▮▮▮"
  "▮▮▮▮▮▮ said the boy, ▮▮▮▮▮▮"

Q. *What has six legs and eats pussy?*

A. *You, Me, and the Lesbian next door.*

I'M BEGINNING TO THINK THAT YOU'RE BEYOND HOPE!

**An Aussie stockman in the outback
was having a pee when he was bitten
by a snake, on the end of his dick.**

His mate jumped on his horse and rode
ten miles to the nearest radio.

**There he called the flying doctor for advice.
"What you have to do is to get a very sharp knife,
make an incision and suck out the poison."**

Jumping back on his horse,
he galloped back to his mate

**"What did the doctor say?" He asked hopefully.
"He says you're gonna die!"**

This one is just too tasteless. Ed.

Maggie put 'Rest in Peace

This one is just too tasteless. Ed.

Q. **What animal has a cunt half-way up its back?**

62

A. **A police horse!**

Then there was the fellow who got fired from Sainsbury's for putting his prick in the bacon-slicer. She got fired too!

A white man stood in a gents toilet, cha____d to
glance down at the ce_____who
was standing n_____.

"M_____. he exclaimed in admiration. "How
do you blokes manage to get such b_____nes?"

"W__," s_i_ the bl_ck man. When we a__ _____ng
our m__h_ers t__a p___e o_ strin_ t_ our too_,
the _ _ le_ a__ch a h_a_y stone to the string.
Eventually that stretches our cocks."

"D_ __ __ow, I think I'll try that!" announced
the white ma__._____

A couple of month_ _____
ag___ _n _he _ame toilet.

Brian Johnston commentating at Lords:
"There's Neil Harvey at leg slip,
with his legs wide apart,
waiting for a tickle".

Two golfers were waiting their turn on the tee,
when a naked woman ran across the fairway
and into the woods.

A couple of minutes later she was followed
by two men in white coats and another bloke
carrying two buckets of sand.
Finally followed a little old man, bringing up the rear.

The two golfers caught him and demanded to know
what was going on.
"Well, she's a nymphomaniac from that asylum
over there," the little man pointed out.
"She keeps trying to escape.
"We are all asylum attendants, trying to catch her."

"What about the guy with the buckets of sand?"
The little man smiled.
"That's his handicap.
He was the one that caught her last time!"

Q. Why are the men in Wales wearing kilts?

A. Because the sheep run away when they hear the sound of a zip!

"Did you hear that old blind Charlie has taken up parachuting?"
"Good Lord. How does he know when he is near to the ground?"
"The Guide Dog's lead goes slack."

Liza: "Rastus, if you stand that close to the edge of the track, a train gonna come and suck you right off!"

Rastus: "That'll do nicely . . . When's it comin' Moma!"

What about the West Indian who did time
for indecent exposure.
He went into Boots to buy some film.
The girl at the counter said:
"What size is your brownie?"
So he showed her!

An Englishman, an Irish... an ... an
were having drink ... to ... ...
into each ... ...
rem... ... ...

th... ... ... it
on th...
Th... ...ed his—and
wing... ...
afte... ...week, he had dealt seventeen

Bush and Gorbachev, having long since died,
were summoned before St. Peter, who said to them:
"You have both made such a contribution to the new
world that I am going to give you a treat.
"In 100 years time I am going to let you go back
for a short visit."
When the time came, they suddenly found themselves
sitting in a hotel lobbly.
Eagerly they picked up newspapers.

Gorbachev laughed. "Hey George," he said.
"It says here that the US dollar is worth 3 pfennigs."
"What about these riots," said Bush, laughing.
"What riots?" asked Gorby.
"The riots on the German-Chinese border!"

And Trevor Bailey:
"Of course I am a great
Willey supporter!"

Terry Wogan: "Tell us something about your wartime exploits."

Guest: "Ja, I vos in the Dutch Air Force and fought the Luftwaffe. When Holland was defeated I escaped to England and joined ze RAF and flew Spitfires in the Battle of Britain."

Terry Wogan: "Could you tell us about some of the action you saw?"

Guest: "Vun day, I found myself alone in the sky in my Spitfire. Suddenly I see many fokkers. Zo, alone I dive at zem. Rat-a-tat-tat, vun fokker, rat-a-tat-tat, anozzer fokker, rat-a-tat-tat, anozzer fokker . . . ."

Terry Wogan: "I think I should explain to the viewers that the Focke-Wulf was a type of German fighter plane."

Guest: "Ja, but zese fokkers vere Messerschmidts!"

The other smallest book
in the world:
"The Irish Book of Knowledge".

Yet another smallest book
in the world:
"Art & Culture in Australia".

A usually forgetful husband came home on his wedding anniversary, carrying a huge bunch of flowers for his wife.

Normally, she was not a very passionate woman, but when he returned to the lounge she was lying on the sofa, stark naked and with her legs wide apart.

"This is for the flowers darling!" she exclaimed.

"Why?" he wanted to know.

"Haven't we got a vase?"

On his twenty-fifth wedding anniversary, Solly's wife cooked him a romantic dinner.

He gave her a diamond ring and said:

"Ruth, you have been such a good wife to me. Is there anything that you would really like?"

"Solly," she said. "When we married, you insisted that we each have a locked, private drawer in our bedside cabinets. As a special treat, will you let me see what you keep in yours?"

Solly took her to the bedroom and unlocked the drawer. Inside she found four golf balls and £800 in fivers. She asked Solly what this meant.

"If you really must know," he told her, "each time I was unfaithful to you, I put a golf ball in the drawer".

"I suppose after twenty-five years, I can't complain about just four golf balls," she said. "But what about the £800?"

"Well," said Solly. "Every time I get a dozen golf balls, I sell them for a fiver!"

Questionnaire:

Give the colour and occupation of the following:

1. Al Capone — White Gangster
2. Stevie Wonder — Black Singer
3. Doctor Crippen — White Murderer
4. Diana Ross — Black Singer
5. Cynthia Payne — White Madame
6. Karel Wojtyla — ?
7. Mike Tyson — Black Boxer
8. The Kray Twins — White Crooks
9. Christine Keeler — White Prostitute
10. Kim Philby — White Spy

Congratulations! You know all the pop-singers, the biggest gangsters, murderers, prostitutes, crooks, fighters and spies, but you don't know poor old Karel Wojtyla — He's the Pope you plonker!

Some years before the war, a man in
Vancouver, Canada, received a telegram
from a good friend in London.
The message read: 'My son arriving
at Halifax on Queen Mary
next Saturday, please meet him'.
The reply came back:
"You meet him, you're nearer!"

74

Q. **Why does a Lada have a heated
rear windscreen?**
A. **To keep your hands warm
when you are pushing it!**

A rep called into a quite country pub
and sat down with his pint.
He noticed a lot of marks carved into the table.
Each mark carrying initials above it.
Intrigued — he asked the landlord to explain.
"Well sir," said the landlord.
"Our locals have a sort of championship. You pop your
manhood onto the table and mark how far it reaches.
They all put ten quid in the pot. At the end of the year the
winner takes all.
In fact today is the day that the prize is awarded."
"Looking at that," remarked the rep,
"I reckon I stand a chance.
Here's my ten quid."

Taking out his prick he rubbed it into a cheerful erection
and then slapped it onto the table;
proudly marking its length on the wood.
"There you are landlord," he said.
"A clear winner don't you think?"
" 'fraid not sir," said the landlord, pocketing the money.
"You see all our blokes do it from the
other side of the table!"

76

Two old ladies about to
have their photographs taken.
"What's he fiddling about
under that hood for?"
"He's got to focus."
"What, both of us?"

A white man, stood in a gents toilet, chanced to glance down at the cock of the black guy who was standing next to him.

"My God!" he exclaimed in admiration. "How do you blokes manage to get such big ones?"

"Well," said the black man. When we are young our mothers tie a piece of string to our tool, and then they attach a heavy stone to the string. Eventually that stretches our cocks."

"Do you know, I think I'll try that!" announed the white man.

A couple of months later, their paths crossed again in the same toilet.

"Hello there," said the black. "How are you getting on?"

"Oh pretty well! In fact, it's gone black already!"

A conversation at
a motor-spares counter.
"What about a
mirror for a Lada?"
"Sounds like
a fair swop!"

**Q. How do you double
the value of a Lada?**

78

A. Fill it up with petrol!

The young barmaid was ▓▓▓▓▓▓▓▓▓ street
when she ▓▓▓▓▓▓▓▓▓▓▓▓▓ small boys
▓▓▓▓▓▓▓ p the ▓▓▓▓.
"What's this ▓▓▓▓, ▓▓▓▓▓" she asked ▓▓▓▓
▓▓▓▓▓
"It's a ▓▓▓▓▓▓" replied the boy.
"Oh, said the barmaid, ▓▓▓▓▓▓▓▓▓?"
"▓▓▓▓▓▓▓ said the boy, ▓▓▓▓▓▓▓ "

"Do you usually smoke after intercourse?"
"I don't know, I've never looked!"

"Before I pass sentence on you," said the judge.
"Is there anything that you wish to say?"
"Fuck all m'lord," replied the prisoner.
"What did he say?" said the judge to the clerk of the court.
"Fuck all m'lord," answered the clerk.
"Don't be a cunt," said the judge.
"I saw his lips move!"

In an Australian Disco:
Bruce: "You're a nice looking
Sheila, do you fuck?"
Sheila: "I do for a smooth-talking
bastard like you!"

A man went into a tailor's shop with a small boy in tow
"I wanna suit for little Luigi here witha the bigga head."

No sooner were the words out of his mouth than
he slapped the small boy smartly around the head.

"Anna then,"
"I wanna some shirtsa for little
Luigi here with the bigga head."

Once again he smacked the child on the head.

"Anna then," slapping the kid again,
"I wanna a coat for little
Luigi here with the bigga head!"

"Please! Sir!" Begged the shop assistant.
"It's true the child does have a rather large head,
but why do you keep hitting him like that?"

"Well!" Said the man. "I married Maria,
the most beautiful girl in the whole of Sicilia.
She hadda the *tightest* little pussy in the whole of Italia!
And then,"

he slapped the child vigorously around the head,
"alonga come little Luigi here with the bigga head!"

The young barmaid was ~~████████████~~ street
when she ~~████████████████~~ small boys
~~████████████~~ up the ~~██████~~.
"What's this ~~████████~~?" she asked ~~████~~
~~████~~
"It's a ~~████████~~" replied the boy.
"Oh, said the barmaid, ~~████████████~~?"
"~~████████~~ 'said the boy, ~~████████~~"

Doctor: **"I can't diagnose your trouble, it's probably drink."**

Patient: **"OK, I'll come back when you're sober!"**

Researcher: *"Do you use Vaseline at all?"*
Housewife: *"Yes, we use it for all sorts of things!"*
Researcher: *"Could you give me some examples?"*
Housewife: *"We use it for medication when the kids scrape their knees, my husband uses it for his car battery to prevent corrosion, and, of course, we use it for sex!"*
Researcher: *"Oh! How exactly do you use it for sex?"*
Housewife: *"We put it on the bedroom door handle, to keep the kids out!"*

Two Irishmen out looking for work saw a sign on a farm gate:

"TREE FELLERS WANTED!"

As Seamus observed: "Tis a pity there's only the two of us!"

"Is that Dublin two, double two, double one?"
"No, this is Dublin two, double two, double two."
"I'm sorry to have bothered you."
"That's all right, the phone was ringing anyway!"

Him: "You'll have to excuse me . . .
but I'm afraid I haven't had much
success with girls . . .
. . . I rather hoped that we could
. . . spend a little time together."
Her: "Your place or mine?"
Him: "Oh well, if you're gonna argue
about it, you can fuck off!"

What about the Irishman who saw a
leprechaun who offered him two wishes.
With his first wish, the man asked for a
never-ending bottle of Guinness. It
immediately appeared in his hand, so he
took a deep swig. The bottle immediately
filled up again. The man was so impressed
that when the leprechaun offered him his
second wish, the Irishman asked for
another one.

After their spectacularly successful six-day war, the Israelis received a letter from the American Administration, offering to swop three US generals for one Israeli general.

The Israelis replied immediately that they would swop their General Moshe Dyan for General Electric, General Dynamics and General Motors!

Girl:
"Do you wear
anything under
your kilt Jimmy?"

Jock:
"Put yer hand
up there lassie
and find out!"

Girl:
"Och, it's gruesome!"

Jock:
"Aye, and it'll
grew some
more if you
hang on to it!"

"I saw you going home with Alice last night,
you naughty boy!"
"So what?"
"Well, I hope you took precautions,
she's got five kids already!"
"Of course I took precautions.
I strapped a plank across my arse
to stop myself from falling in!"

Q. What's the difference between a
mountain goat and a goldfish?
A. One mucks about in a fountain.
The other . . . .

Lorry Driver: "I picked up this witch today.
I knew she was a witch 'cos
as soon as she put her hand on my thigh,
I turned into a lay by!"

He: "If I offered you a million pounds, would you sleep with me?"

She: "Of course I would!"

He: "What if I offered you ten thousand pounds?"

She: "Certainly!"

He: "What if I offered you ten pounds?"

She: "What sort of girl do you think I am?"

He: "We've already established that. Now we're just haggling over the price!"

89

His Lordship: **"Now look here, we have to economise. If you were any good in the kitchen, I could get rid of the cook!"**

Her Ladyship: **"So what? — If you were any good in bed, we could get rid of the chauffeur!"**

A drunk in a pub called the landlord over.
"Tell me squire, do lemons have legs?"
"Of course they don't," said the landlord.
"I was afraid of that," said the drunk.
"That means I've just squeezed your
canary in my drink!"

Disgusting

Two jews were walking down an alleyway, when they were confronted by a bunch of skinheads.

"Abie, do you think we are going to get mugged?"

"Hymie, I *know* we are going to get mugged, Here's the fifty quid I owe you!"

Standing in the queue at the gates of heaven with his wife, our man heard St. Peter reviewing the new arrivals ahead.

"You loved money so much," St. Peter was saying to one man, "that you even called your wife Penny. "Sorry, you're rejected."

"And you loved jewellery so much that you even called your wife Ruby," he said to the next man. "Sorry, you're rejected too."

Our man turned to his wife:
"Come on Fanny,
I think we are wasting our time here!"

One day the Seven Dwarves took a trip into the nearby town.

They walked up to the Nunnery and, whilst the other six stood back, Dopey walked up to the door and rang the bell.

The door creaked open and the Mother Superior's face peered out.

"Yes, " she said, "Can I help you?"

"Errm," said Dopey. "Do you have any Dwarf Nuns here?"

"No, we don't," came the reply.

The other six Dwarves started to snigger.

"Are there any Dwarf Nuns in this town at all?" asked Dopey.

Again the Mother Superior replied "No".

And the other six Dwarves giggled.

Nervously, Dopey asked: "Are there any Dwarf Nuns anywhere in this country?

"No, there aren't," she said. "Why do you ask?"

And the other six Dwarves all sang in unison:

DOPEY FUCKED A PENGUIN!
DOPEY FUCKED A PENGUIN!

The Motto of the British SAS is:
'Who Dares Wins'
The Motto of the Italian SAS is:
'Who Cares Who Wins?'

I felt about as welcome as:
A FART IN A SPACESUIT

93

"How did a struggling young
actress like you get a car like
that?" asked the mother.

"I stopped struggling,"
replied the daughter.

A young bimbo managed to cover up her rather colourful past and married the local vicar.

On their wedding night the vicar went to the bathroom.

She draped herself across the bed.

When her new husband appeared, he said:

"Really my dear, I expected to see you on your knees beside the bed!"

"Naa . . . I don't like it like that,"
"It always makes me fart!"

Max Robertson, commentating
for BBC radio once said:

*"People behind
Martina Navratilova
at the roller end,
have the best view
of her receiving service!"*

Van der Moewe had never been out of South Africa before and was visiting Bondi Beach.

He spotted a long line of black dots out in the water and said to an Aussie, who was sitting close by.

"Vot're all those liddle black things out there?"

"They're buoys," said the Aussie.

"Boys!" replied Van der Moewe. "Vot they doing out there?"

"Holding up the shark nets," the Aussie told him.

"Great country this!" said the South African, deeply impressed.

"We'd never get away with that back home!"

Jack de Manio was interviewing a woman prisoner officer, who had been appointed to a men's prison.
"Do you think the prisoners will regard you as a good screw?"

Opening
doors to
the World
of books

Book Tokens

Book Tokens
can be
bought and
exchanged
at most
bookshops